Productivity

How to Leverage the Science of Breathing to Accomplish More in Less Time

(The Productivity Manual for Lazy People)

Francisco Salinas

TABLE OFCONTENT

Chapter 1: Define Personal Success Versus Corporate Success.................... 1

Chapter 2: What Do You Hope To Accomplish Through Productivity?........................... 6

Chapter 3: Achieving Smaller Objectives Can Be Preferable To Failing To Achieve The Larger Ones. 11

Chapter 4: How To Identify Procrastination's Early Warning Signs 15

Chapter 5: Utilize Your Force..............................21

Chapter 6: Conflict And Development........................49

Chapter 7: Increase Your Sensitivity To Your Emotions...65

Chapter 8: Set A Game-Plan..............................68

Chapter 9: Adopt A Disciplined Attitude 72

Chapter 10: The Initial Step Is To Establish Attainable Goals..76

Chapter 11: Levels Of Energy And The Grey Zone 85

Chapter 12: Employ A Methodical Approach. 93

Chapter 13: Early Morning Magic 97

Chapter 1: Define Personal Success Versus Corporate Success.

Success is not limited to running a thriving business. It is also having a fulfilling and meaningful existence. Obviously, the issue is allocating time for both activities. However, it is possible.

According to Renzo Costarella, the first step is to ascertain what is most important to you in both categories. If you wish to start a family, working more than 80 hours per week is counterproductive. After determining what is most important to you, you must establish boundaries. If you want to be with your children, you must leave your business at the office. Additionally, you may group related tasks and work during your optimal performance hours.

Sundays are not solely dedicated to athletics.

Sundays have traditionally been spent with family, attending religious services, or watching copious amounts of football. But if you want a more productive and organized week, you should also take advantage of Sundays.

How you intend to accomplish this is entirely up to you. However, here are some ideas:

- Perform domestic duties such as laundry and housekeeping.

- Run errands such as going to the grocery store and filling up your gas tank.

- Planning out all of your meals for the week.

- Writing down and organizing your to-do listings.

- Taking care of yourself in order to refresh your body and psyche.

Limit the number of objectives you have.

Without a doubt, you are becoming overburdened with the amount of work you have to complete this week. Once more, take a long breath and start narrowing down your list. Ideally, you should concentrate on achieving at least one important objective every day. If an item is crossed off your list, proceed to your next objective.

Consider employing a method such as the 4Ds of time management to assist in narrowing down your options. Here, you would examine your responsibilities and choose which to DROP, DELEGATE, DEFER, and DO. It is an effective method for limiting the number of items you have next week.

Equip yourself with the necessary equipment.

Even with the best of intentions, the only way to stay organized is to utilize the proper weekly planning tools.

Allow for time for the unexpected.

Regardless of how organized and prepared you are, the unexpected is always around the corner. Your child becomes ill, requiring you to remain home; you may also experience a flat tire on the way to work, causing you to be late for meetings.

You cannot anticipate every worst-case scenario. However, it may be less distressing if you reserve time throughout the week for the unforeseen. One such strategy would be to schedule a couple of hours of free time every day. Avoid watching a movie during this time. Use this section to address any unanticipated circumstances.

What if nothing occurs? Use this time to reflect, meditate, or begin your next assignment.

Chapter 2: What Do You Hope To Accomplish Through Productivity?

Being productive involves completing tasks efficiently. To accomplish tasks efficiently, you will need to be aware of your objectives. It can be simpler to be productive if you have a clear understanding of your objectives. Saying to yourself, "I need to complete this as soon as possible" will not help you become more productive.

Occasionally, deadlines are unavoidable, but you will need motivation to ensure that tasks are completed before the deadlines arrive. Without positive expectations, you will end up living your existence like a machine.

Many individuals appear to value productivity because they believe it helps them pay their expenses. Being more productive can result in increased earnings in less time. Making more money in less time can increase a person's likelihood of paying their obligations on time.

It's nice to be able to pay off all of your obligations early, but it's preferable to have something else to anticipate. It may be more challenging to be productive when your only motivation is to pay the expenses.

Consider your early childhood. You presumably desired to accomplish extraordinary feats and accomplish extraordinary things. Did you truly believe that you would only exist in the future to pay your bills? You probably had plans that were enjoyable to consider and objectives that kept you focused on your vision. You must take the time to regain any enthusiasm you may have lost over the years.

Having a fear of not being able to pay the expenses on time will motivate the majority of individuals to earn money, but it will not necessarily motivate someone to increase their productivity. If we are to make significant progress in our lives, we will require the proper type of motivation.

For instance, a supervisor may scream at an employee to encourage him to perform his duties more quickly. However, it will not be beneficial for the employer in the long run if all of their best employees quit because they are tired of being constantly yelled at.

Failure is more likely than success when the majority of one's motivation is derived from overwhelming pressure and dread. How productive can you be when you are constantly stressed?

Bill payment is a necessity similar to consuming water. No one is particularly motivated to consume water. People consume water for survival, not for pleasure. Because of this, the majority of individuals I know tend to struggle with their water intake. Although it is important to remain hydrated throughout the day, they only consume water when they feel compelled to. They consume enough water to maintain their lives, but not enough to be as healthful as they could be. They simply lack the motivation to consume water.

When you have to compel yourself to do something, you are likely to be less productive. You end up performing the bare minimum in order to survive. Paying your bills will help you get by, but I'm confident you want more from life than just to survive.

Bill payment is necessary but tedious. Consider some enjoyable objectives that you would like to achieve. Is there a particular vacation you've longed to take? Exist any plans that have been postponed due to a lack of time or funds? Are there objectives that you have abandoned because you lacked confidence in their attainability?

As we age, we become more attentive to our numerous responsibilities and obligations. It's admirable to be a responsible, mature individual, but that doesn't mean we can't have aspirations and ambitious plans for the future.

Paying your expenses will motivate you to come to work, but positive, exciting goals will motivate you to increase your productivity.

Chapter 3: Achieving Smaller Objectives Can Be Preferable To Failing To Achieve The Larger Ones.

It is essential to be enthusiastic about your objectives, but it is also essential to be realistic about them. Setting objectives that are insurmountable will result in frustration and disappointment.

It is beneficial to have a large goal that you hope to accomplish one day, but staying focused on your smaller goals can help you achieve the larger ones. Suppose you have a significant aim of saving $1,000. Your secondary objective would be to save $50. You may not be motivated to save $50 because it does not appear to be a substantial amount. However, if you bear in mind that saving $50 will help you reach your larger goal of saving $1,000, you will be motivated to save $50.

If you only have small goals and never have a larger objective in mind, you may not see the value in attaining the small ones. Without ambitious goals to pursue, life can become monotonous. You should have both large and minor objectives. Productivity is increased by achieving smaller objectives on a regular basis, not by achieving larger goals more quickly.

You should not assume a greater risk than you can handle. Without small objectives, it could take a very long time to achieve anything. It can be extremely discouraging to feel as though you are making no progress. If your lesser objectives are achievable, you will be less likely to abandon your larger objectives.

Looking at the distance between you and your objectives can be overwhelming. Therefore, it is essential not to attempt to do everything at once. It is the equivalent of a 2,000-mile solo road journey. It would be very difficult to drive the entire distance without pausing to rest if you were the only driver. Your primary objective is to reach your final destination, but your first minor objective may be to stop at a restaurant for a break. Your next objective may be to halt for gas. The third minor objective could involve traveling to a hotel to spend the night.

If you only set one large objective for yourself, you may feel like a failure every time you fall short. When you consistently achieve your minor goals, it will be like achieving a portion of your larger objective each time. In this manner, you not only achieve smaller objectives, but you also move closer to your larger objective.

Both large and minor objectives balance each other out. Keeping yourself motivated to achieve your small goals by considering the benefits that achieving your large goal will bring can be achieved by considering the benefits of achieving your large goal. Considering the progress you have made in achieving your smaller objectives can motivate you to continue working towards your larger objective.

The idea is to keep your long-term objectives in mind without placing undue strain on yourself to achieve them immediately. Make your smaller goals a priority, as achieving them will make you feel like you're moving closer and closer to the larger objective. Consider the larger objective as something you would like to achieve, while your lesser objective is something you must achieve.

Chapter 4: How To Identify Procrastination's Early Warning Signs

The line between normal and chronic procrastination is extremely thin, as we have seen. While the indications used to identify procrastinative behavior may vary from person to person, it is generally accepted that certain signs are shared by the vast majority of procrastinators. Consider some of these warning indicators.

Lack of Engagement and Persistent Avoidance

Let us examine your existence for a moment. Do you delay important tasks? Before you respond, let's examine the definition of an urgent assignment. Some activities play a crucial role in our overall well-being in our daily lives; this could include a wide range of activities and tasks, such as beginning a weight-loss or exercise program or completing your monthly report. If you consistently put off completing a task, you are unquestionably a procrastinator. Putting off until tomorrow tasks that you should have completed today is a telltale symptom of a procrastinator, a person with commitment (task) phobia, and a chronic avoider.

Bad Time Management

Although procrastination is not a problem with time management, the majority of procrastinators are poor time managers. This suggests that procrastination may be the reason why you are always racing to beat the clock. It may also be the cause of your inability to meet deadlines or arrive on time for appointments. Although time management is not a problem unique to procrastinators, it is a very common indicator of procrastination.

Perfectionism

Perfectionism is prevalent among inveterate procrastinators, particularly those in creative fields. This can occur when you begin an endeavor only to abandon it halfway through and begin another. This procrastination and perfectionism may indicate a lack of motivation and commitment, which is a clear indication of procrastination.

Success or Defeat Phobia

Procrastination is comparable to a lethal dose of the inactive substance. If we were to use the example of a creative endeavor, you might abandon your work halfway through out of fear of how it will turn out. As a sign of procrastination, dread of failure is extremely prevalent.

Illusions of Greatness

The majority of chronic procrastinators are vivid visionaries; their goals are so unattainable that they could easily qualify for the out-of-this-world award. While it is acceptable to have lofty goals, it is more essential to have a detailed strategy for achieving these goals. You will sleep inadequately and wake up a millionaire the following morning, if you have grandiose dreams. Most procrastinators are inveterate boasters; they will boast to anyone who will listen about how "brilliant" they are, despite the fact that they have nothing to show for their self-proclaimed brilliance.

Zap! Energy, passion, and confidence evaporate

In professional settings, the inveterate procrastinator will be energized one moment and exhausted the next. A change in project scope or self-doubt may be the cause of a lack of vitality, passion, or confidence. A lack of confidence in your overall skill is a surefire catalyst for procrastination.

The Acceptance Syndrome

We return to the workplace, where our procrastinator is constantly seeking approbation from his or her superior, coworkers, and group members. This could be an indication of your procrastination or something else brewing beneath the surface if you are in a constant need for validation of any work you have completed.

Concentration Fails to Hold

While concentration is influenced by a variety of factors and situations, procrastination is a major factor in its destruction. As we have observed, chronic procrastinators will typically do anything to divert their attention from the task they should be undertaking. This may involve a consistent review of your email inbox in the hopes of gaining a few minutes of respite from the pressing work you must complete. These small lapses in concentration can lead to larger lapses and, ultimately, the complete postponement of the urgent task.

Ahem! I Am Unable Because...

This is especially prevalent among chronic procrastinators who devise all manner of justifications for why they have not accomplished their life objectives. The inveterate procrastinator will have a ready explanation when asked why they have not completed a task or accomplished a goal. Excuses can take many forms. You may be making excuses for why you haven't started exercising or asked the attractive woman or man next door for their number. You are a chronic procrastinator if you consistently make justifications.

Chapter 5: Utilize Your Force

Not all hours are created equal. Occasionally, one hour is sufficient to complete a large undertaking. Occasionally, one hour is only sufficient to read a few emails.

As a means of increasing productivity, CEOs, performance coaches, and motivational speakers exhort you to identify and capitalize on your peak hours. If you can master a schedule that takes advantage of your most productive work hours, your projects will receive the necessary effort.

The term "improved productivity" is frequently tossed around as if it were nothing more than a buzzword. Exist genuine methods for increasing productivity?

A few hours after consuming a ginseng-infused energy drink or a cup of coffee in the afternoon, the inevitable "crash" will occur. Utilizing one's natural vitality is the key to increasing productivity and sustaining it. Understanding yourself is the key to controlling your energy; you must be able to leverage your body's natural energy dips and surges, as well as these energy peaks when they occur. It is a cycle with a variety of patterns.

Most people attempt to complete a task when they are fatigued and have nothing left to give. They are attempting to harness their energy incorrectly. You may have heard the proverb, "You can't get blood out of a turnip." This is the same as before. There is no water in a barren well.

Understanding your energy cycles and optimizing your energy surges will increase your productivity. Recognizing the times when you are not productive and allowing yourself to take a pause are equally important for maximizing your energy levels. Here, you are not procrastinating. You are merely boosting your energy levels.

Breaks do not have to be at least an hour long; you can take a 10- to 20-minute nap, go for a walk, contemplate, or stretch. Physical activity will distract you from the task at hand if you have a tendency to get caught in your head.

Whatever decision you make, you must be stern with yourself. During this vacation, do not think about your current responsibilities. This is YOUR opportunity to restore and relax.

When learning how to maintain high energy levels over the long term, it is essential to identify any signs of burnout and then take all possible preventative measures to avoid becoming burned out.

Here is a strategy for maximizing your power hours: » Ultradian Rhythm

Humans follow the same cycles as the rest of nature. The amount of research into ultradian rhythms is increasing. The circadian day consists of cycles that last approximately 90 to 120 minutes and occur 24 hours per day. This indicates that each day is governed by cycles that affect our productivity and alertness.

When the cycle begins, we will have greater concentration and vitality. Towards the end, we may begin to feel fatigued and disorganized. If your computer is operating slowly as a result of all the tabs you have opened, you are in an energy valley.

The title "workaholic" may sound appealing, but the reality is that productivity decreases when you have worked 50 or more hours in a single week. Working during your most productive hours may be more productive than working extended hours. This is excellent news.

You must work during your optimal hours, when you are feeling energized and alert, particularly if your project requires you to make crucial decisions, think intricately, and solve problems.

Try to complete these tasks during your energy valley. You will have to battle your brain fog, and the endeavor will be much more difficult and time-consuming.

When you're not engaged or focused, it's simple to complete simple, unimportant, and routine duties. You could still attend a weekly meeting despite feeling drowsy. You may need to support open your eyelids, but who doesn't?

When you know what to do when your next burst of energy arrives, you can be confident that you will achieve your objectives on any given day.

Self-employed individuals determine their own work hours. There are numerous companies that now offer work-from-home options and flexible hours. There are millions of professionals who are able to work when they are inspired, motivated, and alert.

This brings us to the following question: « How can you tell when you are at your most productive? » The Influence of Introversion and Extraversion on Your Energy

You may be curious about the nature of extraversion and introversion. What matters most is how it could benefit you. Here are some suggestions on getting to the bottom of these buzzwords, as well as advice on how to leverage your type.

Let's eliminate the misconception that introverts are shy and that extraverts are outgoing. Carl Jung, a Swiss psychiatrist, devised these terms. "Understanding where you gain the most energy is the key to finding your style and developing your optimal flow," he explained.

Introverts get energy from their interior selves. Here resides their memories, emotions, and thoughts. They experience vitality through inquiry, thought, writing, and reading. Approximately one-third of the global labor force is introverted. The amusing aspect is that they may not appear as they are.

Extroverts gain vitality from the external environment. This is the result of activities, experiences, and individuals. They feel alive when taking action and interacting with the outside world.

The essence of extraversion and introversion is the energy derived from stimulation in the outer or interior world, respectively. Self-Assessment

You may wonder: "I enjoy spending time in both realms. How can I determine which one I prefer?" Every day, we all move between the outer and inner worlds.

The secret is to discover your authentic style and develop your optimal rhythm. Essentially, you must determine where you derive the most vitality.

If you are still uncertain, consider engaging in activities that will either deplete or energize you for an entire week. You may discover a pattern in which certain individuals or responsibilities are extremely exhausting. This is valuable information for you to possess.

According to Susan Cain, the key to maximizing our talents is to place ourselves in the optimal zone of stimulation.

Find activities that transform your inherent energy into pure vitality. Determine whether they exist in your outer or inner world. Commit to observing for the duration, and you may discover that one has more energy and focus than the other.

Now that you understand where your energy is coming from, let's learn how to maximize it.

Support Your Inner World, Introverts 1. Spend Time Reflecting

If your supervisor wants you to generate ideas immediately or someone else requests feedback, you should give yourself time to reflect by telling them you will get back to them after you have had time to consider their problems.

2. Find Time and Space for Privacy

Use headphones with noise-cancelling technology. Find time for yourself at night. Find an office room that nobody uses. Spend some quality time alone with your significant other at home. Allow yourself the necessary time to enter your inner world without interruption.

3. Opt for Written Interaction

It is perfectly acceptable if meetings are not your preferred method of communication. By composing emails and memos, you can capture the energy and clarity of your inner world. When you need to convey your thoughts to others, writing becomes a valuable resource. Extraverts: Seize opportunities in your external environment

Conduct Conversations Offline.

Take the time to speak with your colleagues in person or over the phone if your email conversations with them feel endless. The answer may occur to you during a brief conversation or a coffee run. You will gain vitality from the interaction.

2. Develop Ideas by Communicating

Find a confidant who can assist you in idea generation. They are also excellent for idea generation. You will advance further with this strategy.

3. Position Yourself Where Others Can Interact With You

If you must work on the weekend, consider working in a coffee establishment rather than an empty office. Get off the treadmill and locate someone to run with. Create opportunities that will place you in more stimulating environments.

Understanding your energy and communication style does not imply putting yourself in a box. Many individuals recognize that they fall on either extreme of the spectrum. With time, you will be able to create a comfortable environment where you can leave your character mode behind.

It is irrelevant whether you consider yourself an extrovert or an introvert; you must actively identify and seek out situations that appeal to your strengths.

THE STONY PLACE

According to the parable, the second potential condition of the earth is the stony place. The stony location is described as a mixture of stones and a small amount of soil. The small amount of soil was sufficient to nurture the growth of the seeds, albeit to a limited extent. Additionally, there is something noteworthy about the proliferation of the seeds that grew on the stone. The growth was excessively rapid due to a lack of depth. Finally, we observe that the sun's emergence stunted the growth of the seeds, as they perished due to a lack of soil depth.

Uncleanliness of the Heart

Impurity is the first disease we can diagnose in the stony location. This condition refers to the uncleanness of the spirit of the recipient of God's word.

This indicates that individuals with this cardiac condition receive the word with an open mind and reverence for God. In fact, they accept it with pleasure and the intent to comply. The issue is, however, that they have an impure heart.

If we receive and comprehend God's word, the corruption in our souls can prevent its maturation and fruition. If the word of God is to be profitable in our lives, our spirits must be in a state known as heart purity.

Purity of heart is the absence of evil in one's words, beliefs, and actions. It resembles the notion of sanctity. At this level, however, it is more important to be authentic and devoid of elements that would adulterate something. These may be evil concepts, thoughts, and philosophies that influence our response to the word.

Purity of spirit is the absence of deceit and hypocrisy. A heart of deceit will never satisfy the requirements because it lacks a foundation of godly integrity.

Draw near to God and He will draw near to you. Purify your hands, you sinners, and your souls, you hypocrites. James 4:8

Additionally, the impurity of the heart represents a divided heart. A person who is in love with two different individuals has a divided heart. It depicts a person whose allegiance is divided by other loyalties or forces. It is also illustrative of the person who willingly submits to the Lordship of Jesus Christ in order to avoid damnation, but who has no intention of identifying with Christ's cause.

A divided heart is comparable to a kingdom with two kings, neither of whom can govern the same subjects. It suggests a person stumbling, unable to regain his equilibrium, and unable to accomplish anything of significance due to a divided mind.

People in this category desire God's service for his benefits alone. Such individuals will gladly obey God's word so long as it offers them some benefit and does not contradict their egotistical desires. These individuals are unwilling to suffer in any form. Therefore, when they encounter tribulations and trials for the sake of the word, they are quick to find alternatives.

This demonstrates that these individuals only believed the word for financial gain. They are eager to claim the Scriptures' blessings but reluctant to adhere to the faith's instructions and requirements. Today, there are numerous members of this group in the church. According to Jesus, this can render the word of God ineffective because they only heed the passages they consider politically correct or that align with their ideologies and philosophies.

Lukewarmness

The stony location is also characterized by the term 'lukewarmness'. Although similar to immaturity, this is a distinct form of spiritual heart disease. According to the parable, the stony site consists of both soil and rocks. Therefore, it is neither pure stones nor pure earth, but a combination of the two. This condition resembles the attitude of the indifferent church described in Revelation 3:14-22.

14 "And to the angel of the church of the Laodiceans, write: 'These things says the Amen, the True and Faithful Witness, the Beginning of God's creation: 15 "I am aware from your efforts that you are neither cold nor warm. I wish you were either chilly or hot. 16 Therefore, because you are neither hot nor frigid, I will vomit you from My mouth. 17 Because you say, "I am wealthy, have become wealthy, and have no need, and you do not realize that you are wretched, miserable, poor, blind, and naked." 18 I advise you to purchase from Me gold refined in the furnace, so that you may become wealthy; and white garments, so that the shame of your nakedness may not be exposed; and anoint your eyes with eye salve, so that you may see. 19

Those whom I adore, I rebuke and discipline. Therefore, exhibit fervor and repentance. 20 Behold, I stand and call at the door. If anyone hears My voice and opens the door, I will join him for dinner, and he will join Me. 21 He who conquers will sit with Me on My throne, just as I also conquered and sat with My Father on His throne. 22 "He who has an ear, let him hear what the Spirit says to the churches." '"

According to these verses, persons with this condition are neither cold nor hot, just as the stony place was neither composed of pure stones nor soil.

Lukewarmness is a spiritual malady responsible for spiritual instability and shallowness. It is accountable for convictions' inconsistency. It makes its victims' relationships and interactions with God and man unreliable. The victims of a lackluster disposition will have difficulty standing for a single idea. They are frequently caught between two or more opinions. According to a proverb, "if you cannot stand for something, you will fall for everything."

They believe one thing today, but their resolutions have changed by tomorrow. And this is because they believe and disbelieve too quickly. They are so feeble that they cannot assert themselves on a matter.

What Causes the Lack of Energy?

If we examine why the Lord labeled the church of the Laodiceans as indifferent, we will discover that their true condition was misunderstood. They defined their reality based on what is visible to the naked eye, ignoring their spiritual condition. Christians who are lukewarm dwell in the domain of things visible to the naked eye.

The Bible states, "Because you say, 'I am rich, have become wealthy, and have no needs,' and do not realize that you are wretched, miserable, poor, blind, and naked..."

This results in a perspective that differs from the perspective of the True

Witness. This perception often conflicts with that of the True Witness, leaving its victims in a difficult position. It is frequently the result of differing opinions regarding the demands and requirements of God's word. Therefore, these individuals wish to maintain their opinions while publicly proclaiming the word of God.

Indifferent individuals do not give credence to untrue information. They are believers in transition. They believe anything until something tangible to their physical senses contradicts their previous beliefs.

According to the Lord's interpretation, the stony site represents those who joyfully receive the word until persecution and tribulations arise for the sake of the word. A lukewarm Christian may believe the Bible until something contradicts it. They are believers whose convictions lack substance. They are persuaded by what they observe.

The Stones – Fortifications

In fact, we inhabit a three-dimensional universe, comprised of space, time, and matter. As believers, however, we must recognize that the true essence of all things is invisible. According to the Bible, the visible is created by the invisible.

We are designed to be living beings. We therefore possess intelligence, emotions, and will. This aids in the formation of our perspective, ideology, and life goals. Through our experiences and interactions with the physical world, it aids us in comprehending situations. Therefore, occasionally we may find ourselves deciding between two opposing viewpoints: the visible and the invisible.

We must recognize that it is natural and requires considerably less effort to believe the visible over the invisible. The interactions and experiences with the physical world shape the natural man's ideologies. Consequently, they are more genuine than anything else.

Our human ideologies and convictions appear to be more substantial because they are derived from physical phenomena. These observable ideologies are the stones in our souls. They frequently present violent opposition to spiritual perceptions. They prevent the word of God from penetrating deeply into our souls. They represent strongholds that must be demolished in order for the word to flourish and affect our lives. We will never delve deeply into the things of God if we only accept ideologies developed from a human perspective. These ideologies shape our souls into stone.

The difficulty is that we must first prioritize and esteem the invisible as more important than the visible. And when these two are in competition, we should not hesitate to jettison the inferior to make room for the superior, rather than attempting to retain both.

Those who incline toward and rely on what they can see cannot be productive with God's word. Herein lays the cause of their lack of productivity, as the visible is fleeting and imprecise.

Reality and Uncertainty

I'd like to share with you something that helped me surmount the difficulty of selecting between the visible and the invisible. It reveals the distinction between reality and vagueness.

To be honest with you, we must be grounded in reality. We must not live our lives in ambiguity. However, the issue is that we have interchanged the terms "reality" and "vagueness" in our utilization.

You must have heard people say things like, "I understand what the Bible says, but let's face reality." And by reality, they refer to the evident; what they can see and what they can touch.

Frequently, what we refer to as reality is actually ambiguity, and what we refer to as vagueness is reality in its truest sense.

The point is that we frequently define reality by what is visible and ambiguity by what is invisible. In the meantime, the Bible states that "that which is invisible (vague to us) is eternal, and that which is visible (real to us) is temporal." See 2 Corinthians 4:18.

To live in accordance with the Bible, we must alter our conception of reality. In the kingdom, the invisible is the actuality, while the visible is vague and subordinate.

This implies that we should define actuality by a thing's existence, not its visibility. Not being perceptible does not make something unreal. There are numerous objects that exist despite being invisible to the naked eye. Changing our perspective in this manner will tremendously benefit our Christian lives.

I appreciate that the Bible states that the invisible gives birth to the visible. This indicates that nothing emerges first in the natural world. Everything we see, hear, sense, and experience in the natural world has a massive spiritual undertone. This spiritual undercurrent is the truth.

However, do not neglect that we must also test all information received from the intangible. Numerous receivables from the invisible are not based on the truth.

According to the Scriptures, truth is a vast island that can only be traversed under the guidance of the Holy Spirit, the Spirit of Truth. The Holy Spirit should lead us to all truth.

We must be aware that 'truth' is another term for actuality. Additionally, we can say that reality is truth and truth is reality. Thus, to live from actuality entails living from the truth, and vice versa. To live in reality is to dwell in the domain of the eternally invisible.

This implies that if we want to live a realistic existence, we must specifically live under the guidance and perspective of the Holy Spirit. The Lord asserted that

He is the way, the TRUTH (reality), and life. John likewise stated that the Spirit is the truth. According to the gospel of John, GRACE and TRUTH emanate from Jesus Christ.

All of these affirm that nothing other than Jesus Christ and the Holy Spirit should be regarded to be the truth. Our ideologies may appear to be true, but the Holy Spirit-dispensed word of the Lord is the truth. It should assume precedence in our worldview.

This knowledge assisted me and, by extension, should aid you in deciding which of two opposing opinions to accept whenever you are in a similar position. You should believe what Jesus Christ reveals through His Word and the Holy Spirit about anything that is not physically accessible.

'Lukewarmness' is the result of our failure to walk in accordance with the truth. This will cause us to lose heart when tribulations and persecutions result from the spread of the gospel.

Chapter 6: Conflict And Development

According to the parable, the seeds that fell on the stony ground grew rapidly, but withered when the sun rose.

We are all aware that the sun is required for seed growth. In biology, we learned that the sun is an essential component of photosynthesis. In contrast, this parable demonstrates a different pattern. The sun was responsible for the withering of the seeds' meager growth on the barren ground. When the seedlings' exposure to the sun was limited, they grew more. As soon as they were exposed to sunlight, they withered. This was ascribed to insufficient depth.

What is the intended meaning? It means that if we approach the word of God with a lukewarm or impure heart, the things that are intended for our development and productivity will instead render us unproductive.

Paul stated, "Therefore, we are not disheartened. Even though our outer man is perishing, our inner man is continually being renewed. For our light affliction, which is but for a moment, is producing for us a far greater and eternal weight of glory, while we do not gaze at the things that are seen, but at the things that are unseen. For the things that are visible are transient, but the unseen things are eternal." (2 Cor. 4:16-18)

I adore this biblical passage beyond measure. It is a cure for the animal psyche. Prior to becoming engaged to my gorgeous wife, I had a "picture" of the person I desired to marry, though I was awaiting God's will. First, because I am a music enthusiast and play a few instruments, I wanted the female character to be musically inclined and have a powerful voice. I coveted a beautiful woman endowed with all physical attributes. May the Lord bestow wisdom upon you! However, I was able to resist all these fleshly desires because I was waiting to hear from God.

Unfortunately, when I finally received the long-awaited gift, her physical characteristics did not match my anticipation. She violated what motivational speakers refer to as "compatibility." We were not compatible in almost every way, with the exception of our goals and medical exams. If I followed the advice of motivational speakers on marriage and love, I would not marry her.

I recall lying in bed on that fateful night and telling God, "I don't even like her, let alone love her." I find nothing about her appealing.

Then, the Lord spoke to me clearly: "Read 2 Corinthians 4:18." I quickly grabbed my Bible, and what I read was like soothing oil for my soul: "while we do not gaze at the things that are seen, but at the things that are not seen. For the things that are visible are transient, but the unseen things are eternal."

The protest ended at that point. When the things that I could not see began to manifest in her life, I became confused and commended the Lord. More importantly, the Spirit supernaturally infused love into my heart. I can only continue to thank God for enabling me to see past the visible. No one knows the future except God. Therefore, you should entrust Him with your life choices.

I told you that anecdote to illustrate a fundamental aspect of the biblical passage I cited earlier. When interacting with God, you must transcend the tangible. Your ability to see beyond your current situation and problems will aid you in surviving persecutors and tribulations.

Again, you would observe that, according to this verse, our modest affliction is producing for us a far greater and eternal weight of glory.

Let me clarify so you can comprehend what I am saying here. By God's design, our afflictions are intended to be beneficial. They work for us rather than against us. But this only holds true if we disregard the visible world. Consider again the following passage from the Bible: "For our light affliction, which is but for a moment, works for us a far more exceeding and eternal weight of glory, while we do not look at the things that are seen, but at the things that are not seen."

Our mild afflictions serve us so long as we do not focus on the visible world. If we focus on the visible world, the afflictions may act against us rather than for us.

The Lord disapproves of the notion that the virtuous will experience no tribulations. The delight of the righteous is that his adversities work for him rather than against him. Therefore, if afflictions act against us as Christians, we must examine the depth of our relationship with God. It is a sign that our focus has shifted from the invisible to the visible. This shift in emphasis generates dread and a lack of physical and spiritual depth.

In a similar manner, the sun should support the growth of a seed, not hinder it. However, if the seed lacks profundity, the sun can be detrimental.

Examining the invisible is a fundamental strategy for profiting from the tribulations and persecutions that result from God's word. We must learn to perceive the unseen. We must learn to perceive the unseen realities revealed in God's word. Again, the fact that the Bible instructs us to consider the unseen indicates that they exist and are real.

The focus of tribulations and persecutions is on the visible world. Observing visible objects only weakens us and strengthens our circumstances. Our frailty causes us to lose hope in the face of adversity. "Your strength is diminished if you faint in times of adversity." Proverbs 24:10.

No Depth

We must also contemplate one additional point from this section of the parable. The Lord stated that the seed withered when the sun rose due to its lack of substance. In the interpretation, the Lord ascribed this to a lack of depth and insufficient endurance.

We can infer that patience and longsuffering are also essential for surviving trials and persecutions. The Christian journey is comparable to a marathon; it requires endurance.

In Hebrews 12:1-2, the Bible reveals the secret to pursuing our race with perseverance.

"Therefore, since we are surrounded by such a great cloud of witnesses, let us also lay aside every weight and the sin that so easily entangles us, and let us run with endurance the race that is set before us, 2 looking unto Jesus, the author and finisher of our faith, who for the joy that was set before Him endured the cross, despising the shame, and has taken His seat at the right hand of the throne of God."

In the passage above, the author explains in greater detail how Christians should rush to receive the reward. Here, we might say that the price is productivity, but the ultimate price is the crown we will receive at the conclusion of our earthly race.

First, he made us aware that we are surrounded by a multitude of witnesses. These are the angels who have completed the race successfully before us.

According to the parable, the seeds that landed on the unyielding ground grew rapidly, but died when the sun rose.

It is common knowledge that a seed requires sunlight to develop. The sun is a crucial factor in photosynthesis, according to our biology education. In contrast, we observe a distinct pattern in this parable. The sun was responsible for the wilting of the tiny seedlings that sprouted on the rocky ground. When their exposure to sunlight was limited, the seeds grew more. They withered as soon as they were exposed to sunlight. This was explained by a paucity of depth. What exactly does that mean? It means that if we maintain a lukewarm or impure heart toward the word of God, the things that are intended for our development and productivity will be the things that make us unproductive.

Paul stated, "Therefore, we do not lose courage. Despite the fact that our outer man is perishing, our inner man is being continually renewed. For our light affliction, which is but for a moment, is producing for us a far greater and eternal weight of glory, while we do not gaze at the things that are seen, but at the things that are not seen. For the things that can be seen are transient, but the things that cannot be seen are eternal." (First Corinthians 4:16-18)

I absolutely adore this biblical passage. This is a treatment for the animal psyche. Prior to becoming engaged to my beloved wife, I had a "picture" of the person I would have liked to marry, though I was waiting on God's will. First, because I'm a music enthusiast and play a few instruments, I wanted the female character to be musically inclined and have a deep voice. I coveted a beautiful woman endowed in every way. May the Lord bless you with wisdom! The fact that I was waiting to hear from God, however, gave me the fortitude to resist all those fleshly desires.

When I finally received the long-awaited gift, I was disappointed to discover that her physical attributes did not match my expectations. She violated the concept that motivational presenters refer to as "compatibility." Except for purpose and medical exams, we were not compatible in almost every way. If I were to heed the advice of marriage and love motivational speakers, I would not be interested in her.

I recall lying in my bed on that fateful night and telling God in no uncertain terms, "I don't even like her, much less love her." I find nothing appealing about her.

Then, the Lord spoke to me directly, telling me to read 2 Corinthians 4:18. I quickly grabbed my Bible, and what I read was like soothing oil to my soul: "while we do not look at the things that are seen, but at the things that are not seen." For the things that can be seen are transient, but the things that cannot be seen are eternal."

That concluded the demonstration. In the end, when the things that I could not see manifested in her life, I became perplexed and thanked the Lord. In addition, the Holy Spirit supernaturally infused love into my heart. I can only perpetually give thanks to God for helping me to see beyond the visible. God alone has absolute knowledge of the future. Therefore, you should place your life decisions in His hands.

This story was told to illustrate a fundamental aspect of the biblical passage I cited earlier. When dealing with God, you must learn to look past the corporeal. Persecutions and trials will be more manageable if you are able to see beyond your current circumstances and problems.

Again, you would observe that our light affliction is producing for us a far greater and eternal weight of exaltation, according to this passage of Scripture.

Allow me to clarify so that you can comprehend what I am saying. God intends for our sufferings to benefit us. They are on our side, not against us. This is true, however, only if we disregard the visible world. Consider again the following verse from the Bible: "For our light affliction, which is but for a moment, works for us a far more exceeding and eternal weight of glory, while we do not look at the things that are seen, but at the things that are not seen."

Our minor afflictions are beneficial to us so long as we do not focus on the visible world. If we focus on the things that we can see, the afflictions may operate against us instead of for us.

The Lord disapproves of the idea that the virtuous will not endure afflictions. The happiness of the righteous is that his afflictions work in his favor, not against him. As a result, if afflictions act against us as Christians, we must examine the depth of our relationship with God. It indicates that we have shifted our focus from the intangible to the tangible. This shift in emphasis induces dread, a lack of physical and spiritual depth, and a lack of fortitude.

In a similar manner, the sun should promote, not inhibit, the growth of a seed. However, the sun can act against the seed if it lacks depth.

Taking advantage of the tribulations and persecutions that result from the preaching of God's word requires a fundamental focus on the unseen. We must develop the ability to see the unseen. God's Word reveals unseen truths that we must learn to perceive. Again, the fact that the Bible instructs us to consider things that cannot be seen demonstrates that they are real and exist.

The focus and sustenance of tribulations and persecutors is on the visible. Observing the visible world only weakens us and strengthens our conditions. In the face of adversity, our frailty causes us to abandon hope. "Your strength is limited if you become faint in times of difficulty." Proverbs 24:10.

No Depth

This section of the parable requires one more consideration. According to the Lord, the seed withered when the sun rose because it lacks substance. In the interpretation, the Lord ascribed this to a lack of endurance due to shallowness.

We can infer that patience and longsuffering are also essential to surviving trials and persecutions. The

Christian journey is comparable to a marathon; perseverance is required.

Hebrews 12:1-2 provides us with the key to conducting our race with perseverance.

"Therefore, since we are surrounded by such a great cloud of witnesses, let us also lay aside every weight, and the sin that so easily entangles us, and let us run with endurance the race that is set before us, 2 looking unto Jesus, the author and finisher of our faith, who for the joy that was set before Him endured the cross, despising the shame, and has taken His seat at the right hand of the throne of God."

In the passage above, the author provides a further explanation of how Christians should run in order to receive the reward. Here, we might say that the cost is productivity, but the ultimate cost is the crown we will receive at the conclusion of our earthly race.

First, he made us aware of the multitude of witnesses who surround us. These are the saints who ran the race before us with triumph.

Chapter 7: Increase Your Sensitivity To Your Emotions

Often, you may be less productive at work and in life due to tension or other emotions you are experiencing. Certain occurrences at work may elicit a variety of emotions that reduce your productivity or motivation to complete specific duties.

Whenever you feel anxious or unmotivated to be productive, attempt to take a few moments to determine what emotion or feeling is causing you to feel less productive. It could be a deeper issue, such as an issue at home or a major life change. If this is the case, consider how you can overcome the obstacle and become more productive as a result.

If the issue is more fundamental, you may need to make significant life changes. To be as productive as possible, it may be necessary to remove yourself from a situation in which you feel trapped, such as a job or a relationship.

10. Organize and Prepare

Once you have your productivity tools prepared, use them to remain organized and prepare for the upcoming days and weeks. Many individuals choose to prepare for the week on Monday morning or the night before so that they have an idea of the workload and duties that must be completed.

Organize your calendar and planner in a sensible manner. Due to the fact that everyone's organizational skills vary, it does not need to appear the same as everyone else's. If you're unsure how to create a schedule on your own, you can also acquire templates from the Internet.

Chapter 8: Set A Game-Plan

Successful time management is a characteristic shared by all successful people. You could use "structure," "getting to work," or "a game plan." Whatever phrase or expression you prefer is acceptable. As long as you take it seriously and implement it, you are establishing one of the fundamental principles of productivity.

Consider this and the reasons why it is so essential to success. Consider first the opposite, or the things that do not work. Even if you only have a small amount of work to complete, poor time management could result in it being completed late or not at all. You may have a deadline to fulfill, or you may be working on a project without a deadline.

The outcome will not be satisfying if you do not have a plan for completion. Although procrastination and time wastage are detrimental to productivity, ineffective time management can also be detrimental.

A thorough game plan is essential for increasing productivity and completing tasks. You must first have a complete understanding of what must be done. Second, you must select a completion timeframe, even if there is no fixed deadline. The third phase is putting yourself to the proof by actually doing it. Whether they are short- or long-term, you wish to accomplish your goals. Additionally, you should feel satisfied and glad of the results. Success, pride, and enjoyment are virtually guaranteed when you take your game plan seriously at every turn and refuse to "go with the flow."

Structure and time management may come naturally to you if they have always been a part of your existence. If you are unfamiliar with these concepts, now is the time to adopt them. Whether you are starting your own business, working for someone else, or taking care of your family, developing a firm game plan will provide you with numerous benefits.

If you've ever felt like there aren't enough hours in the day to get everything done, this is a great measure for you to take. You will be surprised by how much you can actually accomplish. With a game plan, you may find that you accomplish more in a day than in a typical week. Each endeavor will be significantly easier and more efficient to complete. You will soon realize the significance of this to your success.

Chapter 9: Adopt A Disciplined Attitude

Self-discipline is essential for productivity and accomplishment. Without it, an individual becomes unmotivated, listless, and dependent on others. Problems with self-discipline can also make an employee, supervisor, or colleague challenging to work with.

The archaic expression for exercising self-discipline is "setting yourself to a task." You must be aware of what tasks must be completed and by when, and then execute them. Good self-discipline requires a fundamental timetable or framework of the tasks that must be completed within a specified time frame. You refrain from becoming distracted or delaying action.

But excessive self-discipline has no effect on productivity. It might even get smaller. You have excessively high standards for yourself if you do not allow yourself any breaks during the workweek or room for error. Instead of helping you accomplish more or do more in less time, it can cause you to become frustrated with your tasks and job.

If you acquired self-control early on in life, you likely do not struggle with it now. If, on the other hand, your family and institutions were too strict or you were not held to high standards, now is an excellent time to begin the practice. You may have survived in your early years without a strong sense of self-discipline, but it will hinder your career.

Recognizing your responsibilities is an excellent starting point for developing self-control. You could begin by assuming responsibility for accomplishing the task accurately and on time. If this is a relatively novel concept for you, you must also accept that errors will occur and be able to rectify them without becoming overly frustrated.

Another aspect of practicing self-discipline is avoiding time-wasting diversions and activities. Despite the fact that you may require and deserve a brief respite during the course of your work, it cannot deter you from completing the assignment. Developing a disciplined routine will make it easier to complete tasks. They will be completed efficiently and effectively. Increased productivity will bring you closer to achieving success.

Chapter 10: The Initial Step Is To Establish Attainable Goals.

Setting goals will help you develop a realistic plan that will place you on the right path toward achieving your goals or objectives without procrastinating. If you are struggling to achieve your professional or personal goals, you are not alone. It may be time to modify your approach to goal-setting. Effective goal-setting begins with the formulation of specific objectives and a practical plan for achieving them. Using the goal-setting advice in this chapter, you can establish, track, and accomplish your objectives.

Setting goals helps a person become aware of the things that require their attention and functions as a motivator for the daily tasks that must be completed.

If no objectives are set, a person's day-to-day existence will develop in a directionless manner, and they will likely drift through life with no clear direction.

Main Points

By setting objectives, you can develop a short-, medium-, and long-term strategy for success.

Setting specific, beneficial, and attainable objectives is a crucial component of effective goal setting.

Set priorities for your goals and communicate them to others in order to remain motivated.

Assessing and monitoring your development while measuring your outcomes is advantageous.

Why Set Aims?

A goal is an aspiration, desire, or objective that you hope to accomplish in the future. When you set an objective, you actively participate in outlining the steps necessary to achieve it. If your career objective is to become a nurse, for example, you may include training, education, and the creation of a work or study schedule.

By setting objectives, you can develop a short-, medium-, and long-term strategy for success. Defining objectives within a team context can increase motivation and provide a sense of purpose.

If you want to remain on track, it's essential to revisit your goals frequently in order to track their progress. Quantify your progress' results if you can. A long-term objective can be intimidating at times, but keeping note of your progress will boost your confidence as you achieve your short- and medium-term goals. Setting objectives and tracking progress can help your team remain on the same page and work toward the same goal.

Goals require more than just good intentions; they must be defined. Just because you desire to do something differently, such as save more money or consume healthier, does not guarantee that you will change your behavior or reach your goal.

How to Define and Achieve Your Objectives

Select worthy objectives.

Many people set meaningless objectives and then question why they do not experience a sense of accomplishment, which seems to go without saying. Keep in mind that goal-setting is intended to help us advance and effect positive change. If an objective lacks this invigorating and transformative element, there is no point in pursuing it. You will only be disappointed. Starting a business is a worthy, life-altering objective that can motivate you to research business opportunities, develop a business strategy, secure debt or equity financing, recruit employees, and market your products. Returning to school to obtain a degree or learn a trade is a worthy goal.

Determine Attainable Stretch Objectives

Standard advice on goal setting emphasizes the importance of objectives being attainable. Almost everyone is aware that it is futile to pursue an impossible objective. You will only experience frustration and give up. Less widely acknowledged is the notion that your objectives should in some way challenge you. If an objective is uninteresting, you will lose interest and abandon it.

Make your goals specific.

Vague or non-specific objectives are a surefire formula for failure. Choosing to get out of debt or lose 20 pounds, for example, is a positive step, but it does not provide any direction on how to proceed. Consider how much simpler it would be if you knew precisely what you were going to do to lose weight. Therefore, when setting objectives, utilize a method that incorporates an action plan. You will achieve more than you ever imagined possible. For instance, if you own a business and want to increase sales by 20% this year, you will need a strategy. You may need to increase sales productivity or launch a social media marketing campaign on Facebook.

Be Devoted to Your Objectives

You must consecrate yourself in order to reach the goal you have set. Because committing to achieving your goals necessitates writing them down, this is a common piece of advice for goal-setting. Create an action plan outlining your objectives and how you intend to achieve them. Motivate yourself with a story of rags-to-riches transformation or a renowned quote. Recognize that achieving a goal is not an instantaneous process and that you will need to work consistently to transform your goal into a reality. And you must set aside the time necessary to achieve your objective.

Make Your Objective Known

Making your goal public is an extremely effective method for many individuals. Consider groups like TOPS (Take Off Pounds Sensibly) and their weekly weigh-ins. Knowing that others will be monitoring your performance ensures your dedication to the objective and is highly motivating. To make your goal public, you need not join an organization or post it on your Facebook page; having a goal buddy, a single individual who is interested in your efforts, can be just as effective.

Chapter 11: Levels Of Energy And The Grey Zone

I have frequently discovered myself doing the following: However, we have all fallen prey to the trap at some stage. And the productivity sin is not dedicating yourself to the task at hand. Thinking about friends and family at work, or even worse, thinking about work when surrounded by friends and family. Consequently, you lose out on both because you do not appreciate either.

This situation is referred to as the "gray zone." You are unable to concentrate and completely engage in the task at hand.

This also occurs when multitasking, another significant productivity sin.

According to data scientist Pragya Agarwal, the human brain is capable of processing 11 million bits of data per second. However, our conscious minds can only comprehend between 40 and 50 bits of data per second. As a result, our minds occasionally engage in cognitive shortcuts that may result in unconscious or implicit prejudice, which can have profound effects on how we perceive and interact with others. Therefore, it is impossible to concentrate while listening to two or three people converse simultaneously, as it takes approximately 60 pieces of information per second to comprehend two people.

As a result, multitasking reduces your ability to concentrate on your work.

Multitasking is advantageous for tasks that do not require concentration and originality, but a burden for those that provide the most value.

And for the remainder of this section, I'd like to guide you through an engaging exercise that will help you better define and comprehend the gray zone, as well as how to prevent becoming mired within it.

Let's refer to the time you are producing your talent as "talent time," as this is when you utilize your strengths to generate value and accomplish your professional goals. The second is your renewal period, during which you relax, rejuvenate, and refuel.

Please pause for a moment and generate a list of activities. And for each, including all the activities in which you utilize your strength and those that you revitalize with it. You can create a dazzling marketing campaign, a task that requires your primary strength. You can include meditation, working out, and drinking beer with companions on your list of activities when you renew your work permit.

Then, you must complete the slightly more challenging process of identifying the frictional barriers that prevent you from performing those activities with complete concentration on each item on the list. Consider the conditions and structures that will facilitate their execution. Consequently, you will be able to implement procedures that will allow you to perform these duties more efficiently and on demand. With sufficient repetition, they will become automatic and habitual.

According to Aristotle, we are what we repeatedly do. Therefore, excellence is a habit, not an act.

Remember to avoid the gray area once again. To make the most of each day, it is important to identify your skills and activities that provide you with a sense of renewal, and then to develop the mechanisms necessary to transform them into habits. There is nothing else to the Gray Zone. If you wish to learn more about this topic, I recommend The Power of Full Engagement by Tony Schwartz.

In their book, Tony Schwartz and Jim Loehr emphasize the energy principle that time is not the primary currency of excellent performance. They reached this conclusion after working with elite athletes and determining how to attain peak performance at specific times.

According to their research, full participation is contingent on four factors:

Physical Emotional and Mental

Spiritual

Consider the entirety of this as a group of musculature. As you well know, both overuse and underuse diminish capacity. Consequently, uncovering and surpassing your limits should be an ongoing objective. However, never underestimate the significance of recovery. Schwartz calls it revitalization. Sharpening the saw is one of the seven behaviors of Steven Covey. Giving yourself time to recover intellectually, physically, emotionally, and spiritually is essential.

To push your limits, you must routinely step outside your comfort zone.

However, doing so intentionally requires significant effort and is unsustainable. Therefore, you will need to develop a ritual or habit that reassures you that you can rely less on conscious energy and more on automation and routines. The formation of habits was just covered in the previous section, so you should have no difficulty with this.

And now, for this section, you must create a ritual that enables you to effortlessly step slightly outside of your comfort zone, as well as a ritual for regeneration. It is applicable to any endeavor, regardless of size. The primary objective is for you to comprehend how this operates. It may be utilized in all aspects of your existence.

In the following section, we will discuss the Pomodoro technique, one of the most popular approaches to productivity today, as well as flow, a method that all creative minds use to produce flawless work. I hope to see you in the section that follows.

Chapter 12: Employ A Methodical Approach.

When a package is full, deal with it immediately. If your "Store Away in This Room" box is full, place the items temporarily in an out-of-the-way corner or get a second box and label it "This Room 2." Refrain from giving up until the entire room has been reorganized and is ready to be cleaned. As a result, you can now reconfigure the storage areas, such as cabinets and drawers, because everything has been placed in its proper container.

Once everything is in boxes, clean the areas where you'll be storing the items and implement any organizing products you have on your list for that room, such as the drawer dividers and side-cabinet hooks you purchased at the garage sale. Then, it is time to return everything to its proper location. This is when the excitement starts. Take a moment to reflect on your accomplishments. Everything is in its appropriate location because you constructed and positioned it! Zowie!

After sorting, transfer the boxes to the next room and repeat the procedure.

Utilize your "sorting locations" slots to subcategorize.

Sub-file items you intend to file away later in the receptacles you've placed at the appropriate "sorting sites." This strategy moves the goods closer to their ultimate destination and keeps them organized in a single location.

The "later" fraud.

There is a time and a place for everything, including cheating, particularly when tidying the house. Build a second box labeled "Later" and fill it with the items you can't find a place for or decide on until the onslaught of in-laws is finally over and the crisis is averted. Place this emergency "Later" receptacle somewhere out of the way where it cannot be discovered when you're finished. Remember to return to your "Later" box once the coast is clear and deal with those disruptive children inside once and for all.

In this new way of life, you don't need to sift through piles of papers or similar objects to find what you're searching for; you simply know where it is.

Why? Because 1) you eliminate superfluous items and 2) you have a designated storage space for everything!

Chapter 13: Early Morning Magic

If you've read any of the writings of founding fathers such as Benjamin Franklin or other prominent figures such as Barack Obama, Mark Zuckerberg, or Elon Musk, you'll find that they all extol the virtue of early childhood education. "Early to bed, early to rise, makes a young man healthy, wealthy, and wise." The hypothesis behind this is that the body secretes the majority of its stress hormone between three and six in the morning. Some individuals, including myself and perhaps you in the near future, are able to complete a full day's work before the majority of people are awake as a result of the additional cortisol and resulting concentration.

Here is my method for modifying your wake-up time to minimize discomfort.

Subtract fifteen minutes from your spontaneous wake-up time and wake up at that time the following day. Therefore, if you awoke at 10 a.m. and wish to begin rising at 7 a.m., you must begin rising at 6 a.m. Tomorrow, rise at 9:45 a.m., then 9:30 a.m., and so on, until you reach your goal. In addition, as a result of waking up early, you'll likely feel tired fifteen minutes earlier than usual, so if you normally go to bed at midnight, start going to bed at 11:45 p.m., then 11:30 p.m., so that the amount of time it took you to adjust your wakeup time is roughly the same amount of time it will take you to adjust your bedtime. Expect to go to bed three hours earlier if you're rising up three hours earlier.

In college, I used the artificial deadline from chapter I, ESEN, and early rising to earn all A's while spending less than half the time my peers did on their assignments. I'm not any smarter than they are; I just used my time more efficiently so I didn't have to work as hard. I then spent the remainder of the day slacking off, socializing, or paying for my education with the time I had freed up.

It took me a long time to learn how to start waking up early 100% of the time, but that is beyond the scope of this book. However, if you are still having trouble, feel free to check out this resource: http://bit.ly/Discipline180.

- The exercise for this chapter is to determine your typical wake-up time, then subtract fifteen minutes from it and make that your new wake-up time until you're waking up two to three hours earlier. Using this newly acquired leisure to work.

Golden Nuggets:

- The body is naturally at its most productive in the morning. • If you do your work first thing in the morning, you can complete an entire day's tasks in a matter of hours. • With your newly found leisure time, you can earn extra money or take care of all the things you've been meaning to do.

Any male who can safely operate a vehicle while kissing a beautiful woman is simply not giving the kiss the attention it merits. - Einstein

Best practices for mind mapping sessions

Mind mapping, as you now know, is an effective form of brainstorming that can yield astounding results and disclose novel, previously unconsidered ideas!

Here are some suggestions for significantly enhancing your mind mapping sessions:

Erase obstructions

Begin your mapping sessions in a comfortable, well-lit, and distraction-free environment with adequate lighting.

In addition, you will need to eliminate any physical or digital distractions. If you intend to map on a computer, disable email, instant messaging, etc. If you utilize paper, keep your workstation clear of clutter.

Start with a strong thought or query.
What tasks must you accomplish during this session? If you clearly define your objectives in advance, you will be better able to work towards achieving them.

Start with a purpose
As the scale of your mind map increases, allow your imagination to guide the expansion of your map. In other words, do not allow your objectives to become limitations.

Permit yourself room for growth.
Try not to cram everything onto a single sheet of paper. Always have extra paper on hand, and leave ample space between your branches; use these spaces to expand upon your concepts.

Don't spend time trying to make it appear professional

Since you are doing this for yourself, there is no reason to limit your imagination.

Record each and every thought that occurs to you.
You may later alter your mind and regret discarding your ideas if you evaluate them too harshly prior to writing them down.

Color code, doodle, strike out, etc.
Your brainstorming does not need to be organized; consider it art and use it creatively.

Before creating a mind map, become familiar with the materials.
Do not inhibit your creativity by perusing textbooks; instead, let your mind guide you.

Self-Control and Willpower

Do you lack the inner fortitude necessary for persistence or action? You would like to alter certain habits, but your lack of inner strength prevents you from doing so. If you answered "yes" to both queries, you are not alone. There are numerous individuals who share your problem. Fortunately, your willingness to develop fortitude and self-discipline can be of great assistance.

Along with your high levels of confidence and motivation, self-discipline and determination are essential to your pursuit of success. It promotes personal development and enables you to make a significant, positive influence in your life. All of them will assist you in achieving not only your significant objectives, but also your daily responsibilities.

How then can one develop both self-discipline and willpower? This chapter will offer some helpful advice.

Remove all possible temptations
Remember that willpower is a scarce resource. However, it is essential not to

squander it. Each time you force yourself to resist temptation without removing it from your line of sight, your willpower is progressively depleted. The issue is that it frequently requires time to replenish it. If possible, get clear of everything that tempts you to avoid losing your willpower and having to constantly replenish it.

If you need to complete a project for your employer within a month, but you are a TV show fanatic, you should remove any temptations to watch your favorite shows instead of working on the project. You can disconnect your television from the wall so that it is no longer visible. You could also cancel your cable subscription.

If your aim is to consume healthier foods, you should stop eating junk food and processed foods, particularly if you're accustomed to eating them. Put them out of sight and stock your kitchen and refrigerator with healthier options.

This can strengthen your resolve to maintain your new routines.

Enhance your capacity to deal with stress and strain

Developing a high level of self-discipline and willpower requires that you develop the ability to deal with tension and pressure. Unmanaged extreme pressure and elevated stress levels can consume a great deal of your body's energy. This can cause you to make decisions irrationally and reflexively, rather than rationally. You will most likely make decisions based solely on your immediate desires. Consequently, one of the most essential stages in enhancing your self-discipline and willpower is to enhance your ability to handle pressure and stress.

The good news is that there are numerous ways to release tension. One is to pause periodically, particularly when performing a stressful task. During your pauses, perform breathing exercises. Perform these whenever you feel too overburdened by your to-do list. This is a basic step, but it plays a significant role in stress management and willpower enhancement.

Additionally, you can engage in yoga, meditation, and regular exercise. You may also begin reducing your commitments to avoid becoming overburdened by the pressure that typically accompanies them.

Establish a solid plan

When your willpower begins to wane, you can always refer back to the plan you've developed and the objective you've set in order to mitigate the negative effects of diminished willpower. While it's true that even those with the most well-thought-out plans face the possibility of failure (since there is no absolute guarantee of success), having a plan on hand will help you persevere despite obstacles. This means that you will continue trying until all of your plan's phases are implemented.

Eat and hydrate well

You must consume well in order to maintain your self-discipline and willpower. Note that nutrition is extremely important for optimal brain function. In order to maintain a high level of self-control, brain cells require sugar or glucose. If your glucose levels are low, there is a chance that your brain will respond powerfully to immediate rewards. This causes you to lose sight of your long-term objective.

Fortunately, it is simple to maintain a healthy glucose level in the body. Simply consume well-balanced dishes with adequate amounts of fiber and protein. Additionally, it can increase your vitality and mental acuity, preventing you from succumbing to potential temptations and making rash decisions.

Similarly, hydration is essential for overall nutrition. Note that dehydration can impair cognitive performance. Water is essential whether you are in class, the office, or the gym. You need between one and four liters of water per day to maintain healthy mental function. Occasionally, individuals confuse thirst for appetite. Consider reaching for a glass of water rather than a snack if you feel hungry when it is not yet time for a supper. You are less likely to lose your fortitude and self-discipline if your brain and body are functioning optimally. This is possible with a healthy, balanced diet and adequate hydration.

Get enough slumber

Getting enough sleep is necessary for the brain to regulate energy more effectively. It also plays a significant role in ensuring that your prefrontal cortex functions optimally. Sleep deprivation, which typically occurs when a person gets less than six hours of sleep per night, can lead to chronic stress, which tends to harm the way the brain and body utilize energy. Your prefrontal cortex takes the brunt of the impact, causing some areas of your brain to lose control, particularly those responsible for forming cravings and stress responses.

You can avoid this by obtaining a sufficient quantity and quality of sleep every night. Get 7 to 8 hours of sleep each night. Researchers have demonstrated that those who get enough sleep live happier and extended lives. Moreover, they are more productive. This is the primary reason why even the most disciplined and self-disciplined athletes have their own sleep couches. This ensures that they receive the necessary quantity of sleep despite their extensive training schedule.

Adequate and high-quality sleep can also prevent excessive fatigue, which can impair your awareness, reaction time, and damage. It should also be noted that sleep deprivation can alter hormones that regulate appetite. Additionally, this can impair your metabolism. Thus, it is time to develop the discipline of getting enough sleep each night.

Enhance the adaptability of your intellect

Possessing a more resilient and adaptable mind is essential for enhancing fortitude. You can increase the adaptability and resilience of your mind by embracing change and accepting challenges. This enhancement will facilitate the formation of constructive responses to stressful situations. Instead of allowing past failures and setbacks to control you, your objective should be to focus on what you wish to accomplish in the long run.

Make the most of your creativity

Using your imagination is one of the most effective ways to increase your discipline and determination. Observe that your body has a tendency to respond favorably to imagined situations that are analogous to actual experiences. For example, envisioning that you are on a tranquil beach causes your body to respond by relaxing.

Imagining that you arrived at a meeting unprepared for your presentation may also cause physical tension. The response of your body to your imagination is actually beneficial for enhancing your willpower.

For instance, if you're dieting, you're likely to experience more intense cravings and other side effects, such as minor irritations. It is primarily because your psyche can cause you to feel deprived. In this situation, you can use your imagination (imagining the negative consequences of not sticking to your diet plan) to combat cravings and other factors that undermine your self-control and fortitude.

When implementing the advice in this chapter, bear in mind that without self-discipline and determination, it will be difficult to achieve your goals, regardless of your intelligence and ability. You must cultivate self-control because it allows you to balance your immediate wants and requirements with your long-term objectives.

While cultivating discipline and developing strong fortitude is difficult (you can't expect it to happen after a single meditation or relaxation session), keep in mind that engaging in certain practices on a regular basis is beneficial. Attempting to establish more meaningful and purposeful behaviors requires a great deal of commitment, similar to other aspects of life. With strong willpower and discipline, you will find it simpler to adhere to your objectives.

www.ingramcontent.com/pod-product-compliance
Lightning Source LLC
Chambersburg PA
CBHW050259120526
44590CB00016B/2412